Hermes and the Magic Map

Jenny Shann

Illustrated by Jim Starr

atmosphere press

Published by Atmosphere Press

atmospherepress.com

To my beloved grandson, George,
Each day with you brings a new adventure!

Hermes didn't want peas with his pasta.
When Granny's back was turned, he flicked them onto the floor. Honey wagged her tail and cleaned up.
'I saw that,' said Granny. 'Go to your room, if you don't want lunch.' So Hermes went, and Honey came too.

Up in his room, Hermes looked through his cupboard. At the very back, he found his drawing pad. There was a big, shiny star on the front. The thick, white pages were blank.
Hermes got out his magic markers and paint pots
and went over to the window.

Outside, he could see his paddling pool waiting for him. He sat down on the window seat and drew a picture of the paddling pool with a sail on it, right there in his backyard. Still cross about the peas, he painted the sky with fluffy, cotton candy clouds. He drew the grass purple. Yes, purple grass! He smiled at his picture.

He thought how nice it would be if his backyard were by the seaside.
So he painted white sand and a splashy sea. In the sea, he drew an island with a path winding through trees.
There was a cave at the end of the path. In the cave, he marked an X.

'Hermes, come here,' Granny called from downstairs.
She didn't sound cross now. So Hermes took his picture to show her.

'Look!' Granny said. She pointed to the open door.
He blinked. Here was his backyard all right.
But . . .

. . . cotton candy clouds sailed across a clear, blue sky. The grass was purple and there was a sandy beach by the sea with an island in the middle. Just like his picture! Hermes ran outside for a better look. Bees hummed in the flowers growing in the purple grass.

Hermes thought how nice it would be if his friend, Star, were here to play with him.
So he drew Star. This was harder than you think, but he did his best.
And just as he was finishing the drawing, he heard a shout.
He turned and there was Star with her big smile.

'Hey, Hermes,' Star said. 'Let's take a ride in your boat.' They pushed the paddling pool over the soft sand into the sea and got in. Honey wagged her tail. She wanted to come. So they let her jump in with them.

The sea was silvery with white-ripple waves and the boat floated along. Hermes and Star dipped their fingers into the water. Down on the seabed, they could see tiny rainbow fish darting around.

They set off down the path that led to the cave.
At first it was dark in there. But in the gloom at the back,
Hermes saw a flash of gold.
'Over here!' he waved.

They scrambled over craggy stones and found a hoard of gold in a hollow rock. They crammed their pockets with treasure.

As they were coming out of the cave, Honey growled.
There was Drake, dressed up as a pirate.
Hermes and Star knew him from school.
This was Drake who pushed you over in the playground.
He called you 'losers' and wouldn't let you join in games.

‘What are you doing here?’ Drake asked.
‘Nothing much.’ Hermes shrugged. ‘Just looking for treasure. This map shows where it’s buried. X marks the spot. See?’
He pointed to his magic pad.

'Give me that map!' Drake said.
Hermes tore his picture out of the pad and gave it to Drake.

'Okay, losers. Out of my way,' Drake commanded.
"Oh, and was that your boat I saw back there? A big wave came up and washed it away.'

Smirking, Drake watched them run back down the path to look for their boat. Soon they could see it, bobbing away over the sunlit sea.

'Now what?' Star asked. 'I can't swim.'
Hermes looked at his pad. He sat down in the sand
and drew two pairs of sandals with wings on them. 'Try these,' he said.
Honey nudged his hand with her nose. 'You want some too!' Hermes smiled.

They pulled on the sandals and felt the wings lift them up in the air.
They were floating through the sky, towards the boat.
The sandals flew them over the foamy waves and set them down in the boat.
'This is fun!' Star laughed out loud.

The boat drifted back to the beach at the end of Hermes’ backyard
They took off their sandals and stepped out onto the warm grass.

'Come and have something to eat now,' Granny called.
She sat at the little, round table, drinking tea with her friend.
On the table there were peanut butter and jelly sandwiches and fruit
and a jug of apple juice. Hermes and Star settled down to eat their picnic.

'Did you find any treasure?' Granny asked.
In their rush to get away from Drake, Hermes and Star had forgotten all about the treasure. They reached into their pockets and pulled out the golden chocolate coins.

With his mouth full of chocolate,
Hermes looked up at the drifting clouds.

One day soon, they'd go exploring up there, on another adventure.

About the Author

A graduate of Cambridge University where she was in the first year of women students at Caius College, Jenny Shann worked as a teacher and then a lawyer. Now retired, she lives in London surrounded by family and her two dogs. She believes in the creative power of art and nature to inspire a love of learning and is grateful to her wonderful illustrator, Jim Starr, for bringing this story to life.

Profits from the sale of this book will go to BBC Children In Need and the World Literacy Foundation.

About the Illustrator

Jim Starr graduated in 1982 from Carnegie-Mellon University in Pittsburgh, Pennsylvania, with a BFA in illustration. For more than 25 years, Jim has freelanced advertising, corporate and editorial illustrations for clients in the United States, Canada and overseas. More recently he began illustrating children's books starting with *The Great Gold Rush Adventure* in 2016. In 2017, Jim was asked by the White House to illustrate the *Holiday Tour Book*, which was distributed to thousands of visitors to the White House during the holiday season. He also illustrated the books *Big Sam: A Rosh Hashanah Tall Tale* in 2017, *Don't Thank Me* in 2020, *The Secret Santa Club* in 2022, and most recently, *George W. Bush: A Little Golden Book Biography* in 2023.

Jim lives north of Baltimore in Stewartstown, Pennsylvania, with his high school sweetheart Karen, who is an Art Teacher. Jim enjoys walking his dogs Annie and Ollie down his rural road. He is hopelessly addicted to playing table tennis. Jim also enjoys painting in watercolor. He was very happy that the author Jenny Shann liked the idea of watercolor painting this book! Jim's illustration website is www.jimstarr.com. Jim's Fine Art website is www.jimstarrart.com.

About Atmosphere Press

Atmosphere Press is an independent, full-service publisher for excellent books in all genres and for all audiences. Learn more about what we do at atmospherepress.com.

We encourage you to check out some of Atmosphere's latest releases, which are available at Amazon.com and via order from your local bookstore:

Alley: I Have Albinism, by Alethea Allen
Santa on a Surfboard, by Laura Sharp
Lilah Loves Life, by Brian Sullivan
The Christmas Witch, by Jaime Katusha
My Sister is Sick… What About Me?, by Mary Kay and Eli Olson
There's a Spider in My Bed, by Devon Nunnally and Biaina Alexanian
Yikes, I Saw a Barracuda!, by Tamara Anderson
Winston's Big Wind, by Barbara Reyelts
Finnigan the Finicky Donkey, by Ashley Vail
Holidays in Trees: Harvest Festival, by Cammy Marble
I Have Worry Monsters in My Tummy, by Erica Wilson, M.ED., LPC., NCC
The Tail of a Trio, by Katherine Scott
Cow Days, by Christina Warfel
Logan and Lexi Meditate, by Denesia D. Rogers
It's Just a Heart, by Kathy Kay

Milton Keynes UK
Ingram Content Group UK Ltd.
UKRC041145270924
448625UK00002BA/3

* 9 7 9 8 8 9 1 3 2 2 8 1 3 *

RESEARCHING & PLANNING A LAYOUT

The biggest problem with the LBSCR, unless you want to model a real station, is finding somewhere plausible to base your imaginary line. I like to use a real location but one that didn't have a railway but a quick look at a map of the LBSC system shows how few places like that there are. Almost every village had a station or was close to one, the whole area was awash with railways!

I settled on Saltdean because although it's a real place it didn't exist until the twentieth century; it really began as a holiday camp and developed from there. That allowed me to use my imagination in terms of creating a Victorian settlement on the cliffs between Brighton and Newhaven. It would actually have been almost impossible to get a railway up there, the gradients would have been fearsome, but that's the beauty of model railways, we don't have to worry about things like that. I also managed to convince myself that once the branch existed it would have been a very convenient line for giving a test run to newly out-shopped engines from Brighton works, conveniently allowing me to run any type of engine the LBSC owned! Imagination is a wonderful thing.

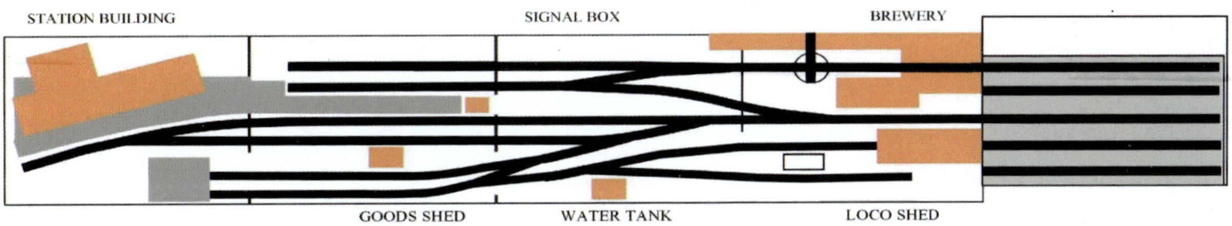

Saltdean is just a simple terminus to fiddle yard layout twenty one feet long, with sixteen feet of station and a five foot fiddle yard. I drew this plan in the early stages and originally the fiddle yard was going to be four feet but I'm glad I extended it, the slightly longer trains do look better. I also put the water tank in a different place; this is how layout evolve, and you never know until you actually build it how it will end up looking. What looks great on paper may look awful on the baseboards, so it will need altering. In my case, if was building it again I'd make the curve in front of the station less sharp but it wasn't until we began operating it that this became an issue, especially with the tender loco's. We all make mistakes, it's how we improve and develop. I do like the station building being at an angle, it gets away from everything looking too straight.

I wanted to include the brewery to give a traffic source and the excuse for a tank engine that wasn't LBSCR, as well as some private owner vans which are quite unusual. No one would ever have built a brewery on top of the chalk cliffs at Saltdean, but don't tell anyone!

Now that Saltdean is complete I've settled on Langstone for my next layout, where the Hayling Island branch crossed the long trestle viaduct towards the terminus. When the line opened for the first couple of years Langstone was the terminus because the bridge hadn't been built, so I have imagined the line staying that way, ending on a pier at Langstone to connect with a ferry to Hayling Island. The pier then developed to serve coastal paddle steamers and a wharf was built to handle freight...lots of shunting potential there.

It would never have happened, of course, but it doesn't matter...that's part of the fun. A liberal

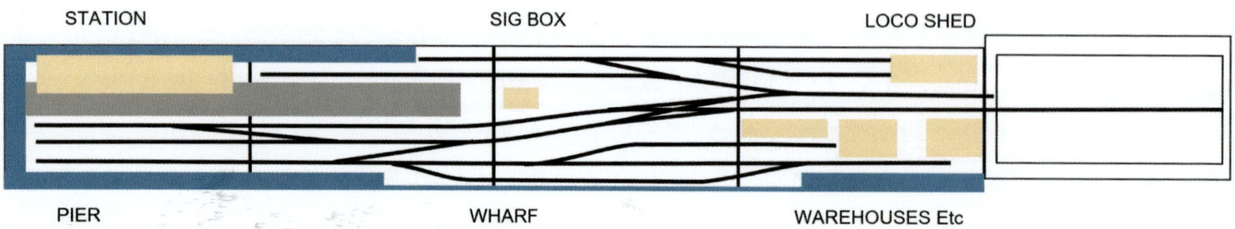

Like Saltdean it's just a simple 20' long terminus—fiddle yard layout, but the trick is to make it look different. In this case the left hand section is on a wooden pier with the water level six inches or so below the track. The wharf sidings take the place of the goods yard and can be shunted without blocking the main line, as can the loco shed with the second track into the fiddle yard allowing the loco's to run on and off the shed independently.

Of course, with Havant just up the road there wouldn't have been a loco shed here but I've got to put all those engines somewhere and people do like to be able to see them.

There is scope for some very enjoyable architectural modelling.

The SECR stations at Port Victoria and Queenborough Pier show the sort of thing I have in mind for Langstone.

I think I'd have to assume the steamer had just sailed, it would be huge in 7mm scale.

Whoever coloured the postcard had obviously never seen a real M3 class 4-4-0!

There are possibilities closer to London if you fancy a bit of a backwater serving wharves on the Thames, similar to the Deptford wharf branch, lifting bridge and all.

This is purely a shunting layout with the fiddle yard on a sliding traverser behind the buildings on the right. The Deptford lifting bridge is on the left with a footbridge disguising the fact that the line does not go any further beyond that. There is lots of scope for architectural modelling, though the height would mean operating from the front in order to reach the couplings.

DEPTFORD "LIFT" BRIDGE OVER THE GRAND SURREY CANAL. Waterlow & Sons Ltd.

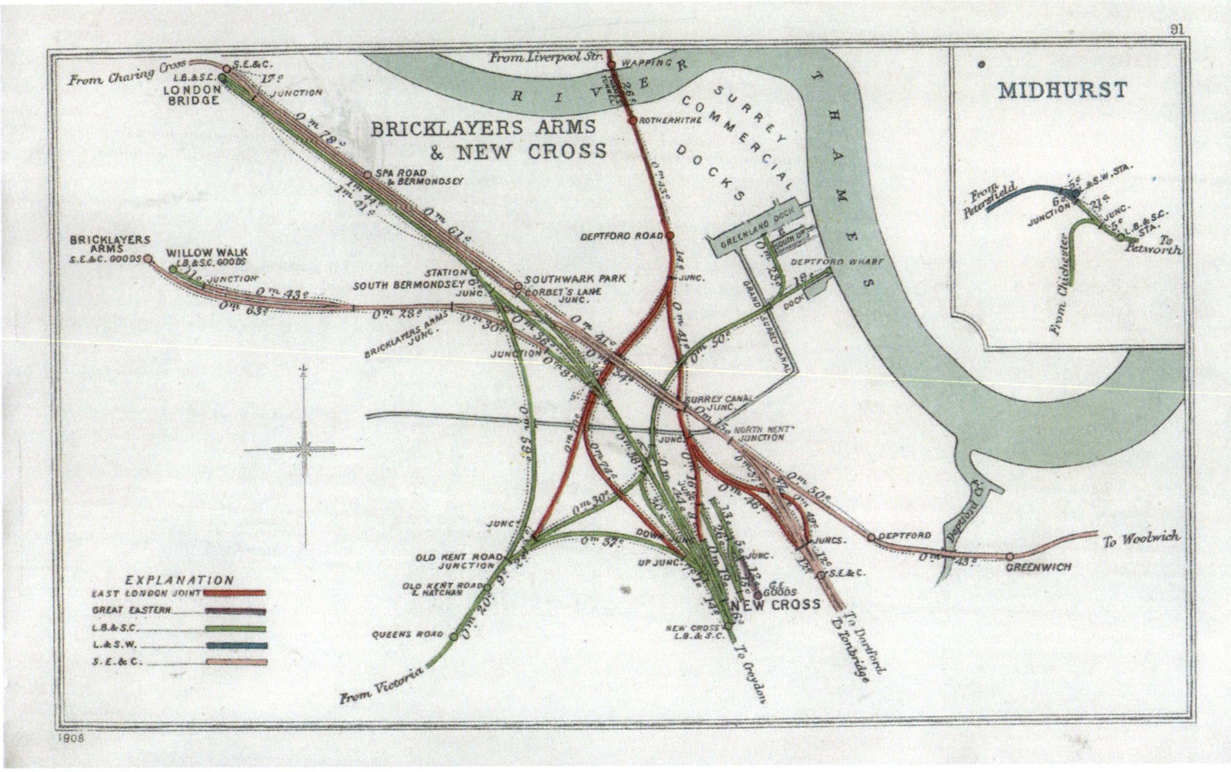

The RCH maps for the two areas in which I have planned layouts, Langstone and Deptford Wharf.

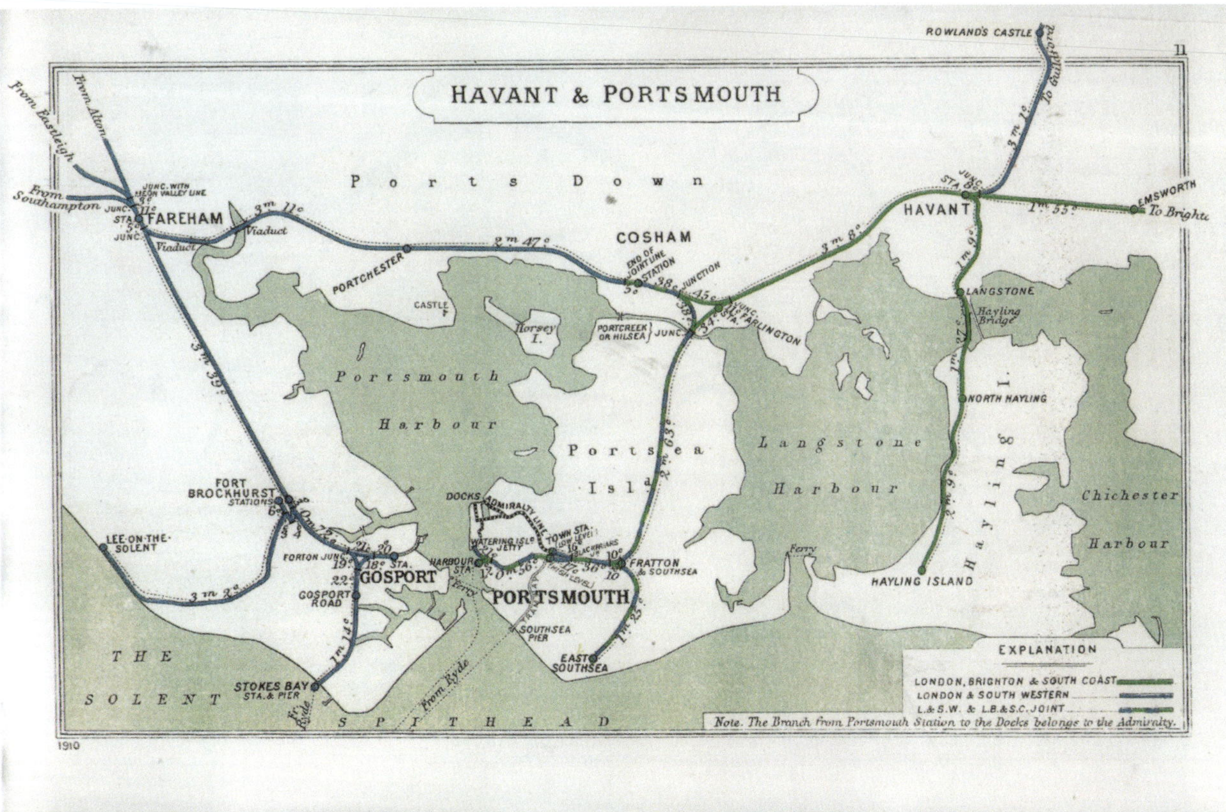

The final layout suggestion is a little different as it is based on a real location, Brighton Works. You might think an 0 gauge layout based on such a vast complex would be impossible but you'd be wrong, it's quite manageable if you focus in on just a part of the works. It's ideal for those of us with far too many engines, of course.

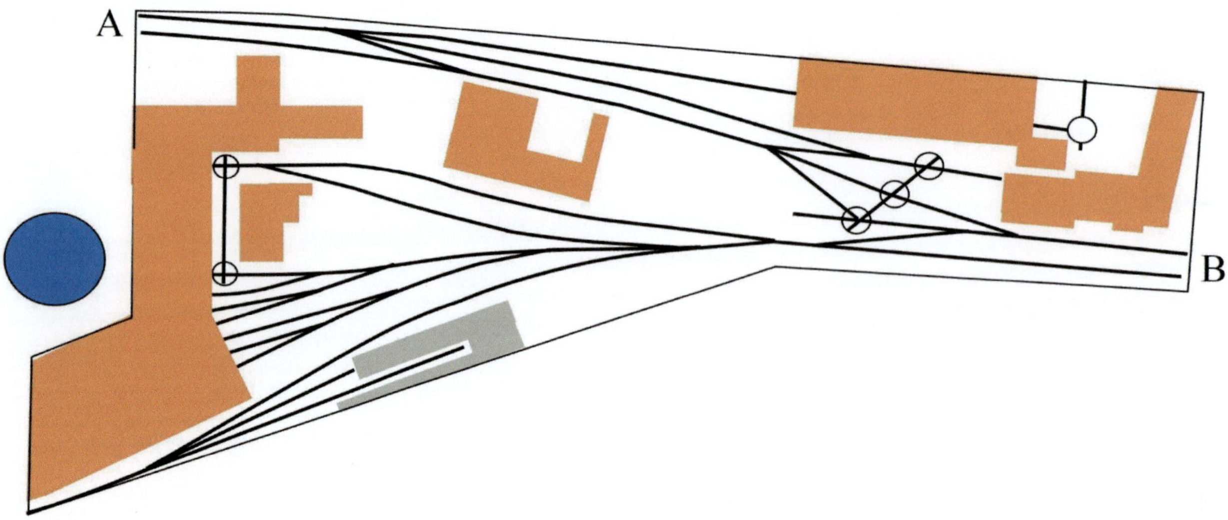

3 feet in 7mm scale

The top plan is very workable but the problem is the width of the baseboards, especially with three link couplings so in the lower plan I have compressed the lines along the lower edge to shorten the layout. The grey area is a bay platform, the rest of Brighton station being just off scene. A and B are suggested operating positions using hand held controllers with long leads. The plan is pretty much exactly to scale; a fiddle yard could be added at either end if you wanted to.

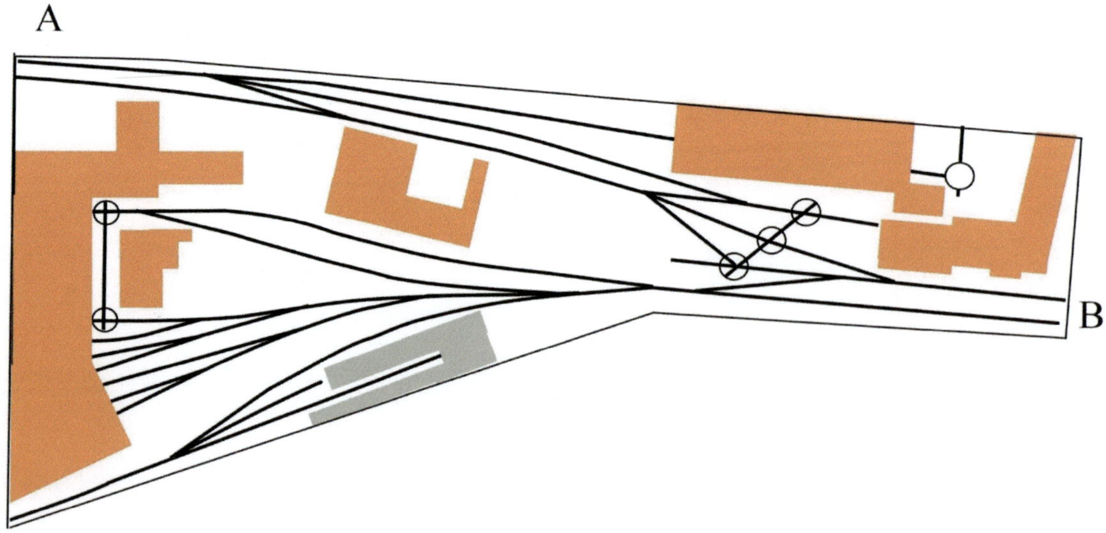

3 feet in 7mm scale

TRACK

There are really only two options available in 7mm scale, you either use Peco ready made track and points or you make your own using C&L components. The latter undoubtedly look better but I opted for the easy route and used Peco, in the main because only the railheads are going to seen. The Victorians ballasted their track so that the sleepers were covered in the belief that it protected them, whereas in fact it was just covering up the rot.

The LBSCR used crushed shingle for a beach near Newhaven as ballast—it was free! Recreating the look of track ballasted in this way is a little different from what is usually done but the extra work is well worthwhile.

The area between the point blades was kept clear of ballast and the sleepers could be seen here, but everywhere else was covered right up to the rail heads. Another advantage of using Peco points on a small layout is that they are fairly short yet the radius of the curve is six feet so trains run through them smoothly. The chairs are much too modern looking for a layout set in the 1880's, but as they are covered with ballast that doesn't matter.

I draw all the main features onto the baseboard with a marker pen before beginning work, just to make sure that everything is going to fit. I then lay the track directly onto the plywood surface of the baseboard.

Shock! Horror! What about the underlay?

I don't use underlay. I used to, but now I don't bother.

I've used cork; it's so thin it seems to make no discernible difference. I've used foam, which is too soft, and Neoprene sheet which is £25 a square metre which is too expensive and again doesn't seem to make any difference.

Underlay is supposed to make things quieter, but once it's been soaked in PVA during ballasting any sound deadening properties are lost, it all sets solidly. I've concluded that underlay is a waste of time and money.

I simply glue the Peco track in place on the baseboard using Evostick, after drilling an elongated hole for the wire from the point motor. At the baseboard edge I either glue down strips of copper clad sleeper strip and solder the rail ends to that, or knock in a thin nail alongside the rail which works just as well and looks neater if the ballast is going to be conventional. Where there are metal rail joiners I solder one side to the rail so the joiner stays in place but the adjoining rail can still move.

The dropper wires are soldered in place and that's about it; simple!

It's best to add the platform after the adjacent track is in place so that the correct clearance can be maintained. I use 1" wood blocks which gives the right height once the surface has been added from 3mm thick plastic sheet.

I ballast the track using Woodland Scenics products, but I always mix my own blend to suit the layout. Here there is a mixture of fine buff, medium buff and medium brown which gives a nice variation to the tone. I put some of each into and empty plastic jar (the ones the ballast comes in, ideally) and give it a good shake to mix it all up. Then it can be used straight from the jar.

I paint the track with a spray can of Railmatch sleeper grime first, and when that's dry the ballast is poured over it and smoothed out using a 2" wide paintbrush. I clear it from around the point tie bar, but make no attempt to keep the flangeways clear on the inside of the rail because as soon as the PVA is put on these will simply fill up again.

Once all the track has been covered with ballast up the rail height I add the diluted PVA glue into which a drop of washing up liquid has been added. I dilute it to around three parts water to one of glue, and use the cheap own brand stuff from B&Q in litre bottles, it works just as well as the more expensive brands. I pour on the PVA from an empty litre glue bottle; forget about adding it a drop at a time, there's a whole baseboard to cover! I keep adding glue until the area of ballast turns white, then I know it's had a good soaking.

After an hour or so it's possible to remove any ballast from around the point blades but that's all, other than that leave well alone and resist the temptation to fiddle!

The glue may well need around two days to go really hard, depending on the weather; I work in the garage so cold damp days are not the ones to choose for this job.

Once the ballast is totally dry and rock hard the tedious job of scraping a flangeway on the inside of the rail can begin for which I use a screwdriver. It's far better to wait and do it now than trying to do it when the ballast is wet which just makes a mess.

The trick is to remove enough but no more as our model wheels have deeper flanges than the real thing and we want our track to look as though the ballast is still at rail level. I use an old wagon for testing purposes. Once it has all been scraped this is the sort of look you can achieve:

I have painted the visible sleepers, added point rodding from 2mm brass wire in plastic card mounts, and a ground signal. I remove the plastic cover Peco put over the tie bar and replace it with real wood strip planking though it is also possible to simply cut away the plastic moulding altogether using a Stanley knife.

Now it's a case of working your way along the layout until it has all been done. I can never resist finishing one board so I've got something to look at while working on the rest of it.

Work on the track doesn't finish with the ballasting, though. Areas where loco's stand need to be sprayed black, with quite well defined edges which surprised me when I saw it at the Bluebell. A pile of ash can be added—just light grey ballast in a heap fixed down in the same way as the ballast itself. The water crane is from Ragstone Models.

This road crossing the sidings was done using fine brown ballast. The static grass is just put in place on the wet ballast using my fingers—there's no need for an applicator.

The LBSC used rail built buffer stops with a wooden cross beam, painted in black & white. Mine are kits from Ragstone Models. It's worth getting details such as this right rather than just using generic ones.

Detail around the engine shed with a brick lined pit in the shed road. The visible sleepers on the siding are dry brushed in shades of grey, and the ballast here is ash. The ash piles are grey ballast dry brushed in white once they are dry.

The track into the brewery yard has cosmetic wagon turntables from Skytrex. The line runs through the building into the fiddle yard to allow shunting without blocking the main line.

CONTROL

I am not going to go into great detail about this because everyone has their favourite method and really it has nothing to do with modelling the LBSCR.

Briefly, I use a Lenz 100 DCC system which I find very user friendly and robust and reliable. The control boxes and transformers are fixed into an aluminium camera box and simply plug into the layout which has sockets for the hand held controllers all along both front and back. The controllers can be held in one hand, leaving the other free for important things like cups of tea.

I use Hoffmann point motors for the points and the signals, all of which are operated from the hand held unit. The speed of the point motors can be adjusted so the signals can be made to move nice and slowly.

SIGNALS

There are four operating semaphore signals on the layout and a couple of ground signals that are dummies.

The LBSC used slotted post semaphore signals until the turn of the twentieth century when the change was made to the familiar semaphores that can still be seen at Sheffield Park station. The changeover was done very quickly, the slotted post signals had pretty much all gone by 1910.

Not surprisingly kits for these signals are not available so a little imagination was called for. Scale Signal Supply do a kit for a North Eastern Railway slotted post semaphore so I used these and adapted them, using a more Brighton looking finial and placing the ladder on the front of the post. The lamp had rotating lenses that moved when the arm was lowered but mine are fixed and are not lit; in daylight the lamp would not have been burning, that cost money.

One thing that made Brighton signals stand out at that time was that the stripe on the red arm was black, the white strip not coming into use until the new signals were introduced around 1901. This is another feature that makes the layout distinctive and people do notice.

The ground signals had red and green discs that rotated to face the traffic according to the position of the adjoining point. It would be possible to make them work but I haven't bothered, there was too much else to do. My kits came from Wizard Models.

One of the four slotted post signals on the layout, showing the unfamiliar colour scheme. It's by no means a perfect LBSC signal but it does the job. They are operated from Hoffman point motors mounted under the baseboard on a plastic mount so they are at 90 degrees to the normal position, the operating wire passing through the baseboard.

My signals only have two positions, like the later semaphores.

BUILDINGS

This is not the place to go into a detailed description of how the buildings were constructed, I have written another book about that (see bibliography), but a few notes specifically about the LBSC models may be of interest.

As I have already mentioned one of the great attractions of modelling the LBSCR is the wonderful architecture, especially the stations designed by Terence Myers in the 1880's. Most of these were on secondary routes and I was immediately drawn to the fabulous station at Lavant on the Chichester to Midhurst line. Lavant is a small place but the LBSC provided it with a monumental station building on three levels that towered above the railway.

One area that can be used to good effect to make any layout stand out from the crowd is through it's buildings. I could have modelled a very conventional small station which would have been perfectly adequate for the traffic, but where's the fun in that?

My model isn't an exact copy of Lavant but that was certainly the inspiration for it. I built it on a separate base for ease of working before installing it on the layout once it was finished.

I use plastic card for the shell of the building, in this case 2mm thick for the most part which is braced inside with strip-wood glued with Evostick. This gives a very strong model but doesn't make it too heavy. The shell is then covered using printed papers which I produce and market.

When first built these stations had plaster panels on the upper walls which looked wonderful but they let in the damp so only a few years after being built they were clad with hanging tiles as on my model. I wish now that I'd modelled it as built because it would have been more unusual but it's too late now and the tiles would probably have been in place by 1888. My tiles are taken from photo's taken at Horsted Keynes so they are very accurate!

The canopy on the real thing was covered with lead sheet; on the model it is aluminium cooking foil stuck in place with Evostick and pressed down over plastic strip battens. It was painted grey before being dry brushed in white.

One feature of these Myers stations is that no two seemed to have the same design of canopy valancing. They were originally very deep but this fouled the SR loading gauge so they were cut back in the 1920's which totally altered the look of the station. My canopy uses my own etched valancing based on the pattern used originally at Sheffield Park.

The mullioned windows use 3mm clear plastic for the glazing which is stuck behind the two layers of plastic window frames. Then the stone mullions are added from printed paper, scored and folded into a V shape.

The brickwork looks so convincing because it is produced from a photo of a real brick wall with all the shadows and variations in colour. Real Myers station used a darker, redder looking brick but on a model station lightening the colour is a good thing in the same way that a grey locomotive model looks more convincing than a dead black one.

The stained glass is from a photo of Sheffield Park station, resized on the computer, printed off and stuck behind the glazing.

The LBSC poster boards are probably a bit too modern for 1888 but I like them; they are my own product.

We are very fortunate that three Myers station buildings remain in use on the Bluebell Railway with Sheffield Park restored beautifully to LBSCR condition. Reference to this was invaluable in producing my model.

I used this picture to model the carved stone-work panels above the window, adjusting the perspective with Photoshop. How convenient that my station also opened in 1882!

These plaster panels give a hint of how the whole upper part of the building would have looked before it was tiled.

I used this picture to produce the curved panels on my model.

All Myers stations had this distinctive porch, in fact some had two.

Similar framing was used on the end gable at Sheffield Park; fortunately on my model this wasn't required.

There is no short cut to modelling the unique wooden canopy supports, seen here on another model in SR colours. I used Plastruct square section and lots of patience. If I was to do another there might be a case for having the parts laser cut to slot together.

Signal boxes were generally small in the 1880's before interlocking came in and required longer frames. For a station the size of Saltdean this attractive little box with twelve levers is fine.

The LBSC used a colour scheme of very pale cream and deep red on buildings— it's possible that the cream was originally white which yellowed a little as it aged. The red would have had a brown under-coat as the colour is translucent, so I do the same on my models.

I always like to model the interiors in signal boxes even though in this case it is barely visible. Making the roof removeable is a good idea in case anything comes loose.

The top panels with the distinctive ventilation slots are printed on matt paper and stuck in place.

The water tower is based loosely on Horsted Keynes; the structure is all plastic and the water is a sheet of 3mm thick clear plastic. Nothing looks worse than bendy water! The plastic ladder has sagged and I didn't notice when I took the picture.

The loco shed is pretty generic and was built to fit the constricted site. The LBSC had very few single road sheds, in fact only Midhurst comes to mind, and in reality a station only ten miles from Brighton wouldn't have needed a shed. It's a useful way of hiding the line behind it running into the fiddle yard.

The brewery is little more than a flat wall but it fills the far corner nicely and gives more scope for shunting and freight traffic. The lettering was overlayed onto the brick paper and then faded a little so the bricks show through.

SUPPLIERS FOR TRACK, SIGNALS AND BUILDINGS.

TRACK

Peco products are widely available from model shops. I generally use Tower Models.

POINT MOTORS: Hoffmann motors from Germany, bought from Aspen Model whose website can be accessed in English and who take Paypal. The motors can be used with DCC without needing any modification.

BUFFER STOPS: LBSCR buffer stops are available as kits from Ragstone Models.

WATER CRANES are also produced in two styles, platform and ground mounted.

BALLAST: I use Woodland Scenics ballast, generally the medium grade.

SIGNALS

Kits for NER slotted post signals are produced by Scale Signal Supply.

Wizard Models produce ground signal kits and components for the post 1901 LBSCR signals.

BUILDINGS

I trade as **KIRTLEY MODEL BUILDINGS** and produce a range of building papers as well as accessories such as LBSCR poster boards. I also build to commission.

PLASTIC CARD I buy this from Stephen Webster Plastics in large sheets—it is called HIPS, or High Impact Polystyrene Sheet.

CLEAR GLAZING This clear 3mm sheet is sold by B&Q under the trade name Aerial. B&Q also sell the stripwood used for internal bracing.

PLASTIC SECTIONS I use Plastruct, bought from EMA Models.

CHIMNEY POTS S&D Models

Accessories for buildings are produced by Duncan Scale Models, York Modelmaking, S&D Models and many others.

LOCOMOTIVES.

The locomotives of the LBSCR from 1870 until March introduced the Umber livery in 1905 were decked out in an eye catching colour scheme that really caught the imagination of observers when it was first introduced. The basic colour was Gamboge Yellow and over the years this colour, often known as 'Improved Engine Green', has reached almost a mythical status with reams written about it, much of it frankly not worth the paper it is printed on.

Before 1870, under Craven, LBSC loco's were dark green like those on a great many other lines; green was cheap, covered well, wore well and was resistant to heat. Stroudley worked for the Highland Railway before coming to Brighton and there he used a Gamboge Yellow livery for locomotives. When he came south he simply continued using the same scheme, except that the spokes were no longer lined.

When he proposed using the new colour, he said to the Board of Directors "I think you will find this is an improvement on engine green', and it has been misquoted ever since.

This is what gamboge yellow looks like:

There is no mystery about it, it is a standard colour used by artists and has been for years.

The elaborate lining used by Stroudley affects how we perceive the colour, and bright sunshine can make a locomotive almost seem to glow; no wonder it impressed the Victorians in 1870 when all they had been used to was dark green.

The colour could change with time, especially in the atmosphere of industrial south London and the varnish used in those days browned with age, but the colour was gamboge yellow. It is

In Brighton Museum is a model of the D2 class locomotive Como which was reputedly painted using actual paint from Brighton Works. It must be right, mustn't it?

You have to allow for the aging of the paint and the browning of the varnish, but even so it's a contemporary source so it's invaluable. However, using the same shade on a model doesn't look the same as the original loco as the areas covered are so much smaller...the colour looks darker. Victorian varnish browned as it aged so Como doesn't necessarily look the same colour now as it did when it was first painted. Even so, it's pretty close to Gamboge Yellow.

A book on LBSCR liveries was published by the HMRS during 2016 and a colour patch was included for the locomotive colour, supposedly copying the colour of Como. Despite the text always referring to the colour as yellow, this is the colour of the paint patch:

Not only is it not Gamboge Yellow, it's nothing like the colour of Como either!

All the contemporary references I have seen are to 'yellow' as are the postcards published by the Locomotive Publishing Co. which were notable for the care they took to represent things accurately. A series of articles written for the Railway Magazine in 1932 by Victor Nelson refer to the engines as 'yellow', as does Hamilton Ellis in his 1960 book on the Brighton. These people saw these engines, they rode behind them. They knew what they were describing, as did the people who first restored Boxhill and Gladstone. To suggest that they didn't use the right colour or description is patronising and insulting....they'd seen it, they remembered it as we remember liveries from the 1960's and 1970's.

Over the years people have turned linguistic somersaults trying to explain why Stroudley chose this colour....he must have been colour blind and saw it as green is one tall tale. Colour blind people do not see that colour as green.

The truth is simple; he picked that colour because he liked it. He used it on the Highland and he used it on the Brighton, where it became celebrated among railway lovers and the general public alike. Stroudley knew the value of publicity, and it distracted people from the underwhelming coaches!

Billinton was no fool either, he continued using exactly the same livery throughout his time in charge. People may not have known much about the Brighton railway but they all knew about the yellow engines.

LOCOMOTIVES FROM 1870 TO 1889

When Stroudley took office the Brighton railway was a mess. Craven had been designing loco's for them for years and no two were alike; even a class of two engines would be different! This is the sort of thing they were running the system with....

Stroudley quickly took things in hand, and from then on the railway was a shining example of the benefits of standardisation. This is a boon for modellers of course as so many of the parts are interchangeable.

When he arrived in 1870 Stroudley found the parts already in the works for building two tank engines, so he had them completed and they did useful work until they were displaced by the Terriers and D class after which they never really found much useful to occupy them. This is a model of No. 467 decked out in the full yellow livery, the first new engines to carry it.

The two tanks were built as Nos 18 and 21 in 1871 and looked very un-Stroudley like although they did have the characteristic curved top to the sidetanks. They proved a useful forerunner of the D class 0-4-2T loco's in that it was possible to test the suitability of the wheel arrangement for use on suburban services. The success of the D's proved the point.

The kit for No. 462 came from Mike Waldron of EB Models who kindly enlarged his 4mm scale etchings leaving me to source suitable castings. My model has a Midland safely valve and the dome from an LNW Coal Tank, but at least the chimney is Brighton.

The large gong was the business end of the passenger communication cord; I set my layout in 1888 by which time it was going out of use but it's too nice not to have included. No 467 was withdrawn in August 1888 so she's on her last legs on Saltdean. I like her, it's important on a layout to have to occasional engine that's a bit out of the ordinary along with the commoner types.

C CLASS 0-6-0 GOODS ENGINES

The first true Stroudley design came into service from 1871, the C class goods engines. They were painted in the much simpler olive green livery reserved for goods classes, lined in black.

These engines weren't a great success initially but they make an attractive model with all the features associated with Stroudley already present such as the distinctive cab roof and the well proportioned boiler fittings. The tender with the underhung springs was his first design; happily he later replaced it with the familiar type with inside bearings which was much more appealing to the eye.

STEPHENSON 2-2-2 LOCOMOTIVES.

These single wheeled express engines were already on order from Stephensons when Stroudley arrived but he was able to influence the design a little before the first ones were delivered in 1870. They carried the full yellow livery from the start and were well proportioned engines, the last class to be introduced before all the well known Stroudley features came into use. My model is of 'Dieppe', the French port to which the LBSC steamers sailed from Newhaven and she is a mixture of etchings from Mike Waldron with fittings from all over the place...frankly, if it looked right I used it. The chimney is Stroudley, one of the things he did manage to get changed.

The tender is pure Craven, again with the large gong to attract the attention of the driver. Despite being very much non standard these were useful machines with a respectable top speed and ran on the main line until Stroudley's own designs began to appear in the late 1870's. The fact that he felt able to concentrate on tank and goods engines during his first years shows that the fast trains were in perfectly capable hands.

I think she's a beauty but it must have been awfully draughty on the footplate!

CLASS B 'BELGRAVIA' CLASS 2-4-0

This class of six engines emerged from the works in 1872 having made use of some parts already on order when Stroudley took charge. Belgravia was built with a domeless boiler but my model depicts her in later years with all the standard Stroudley fittings.

Some of the class used old Craven tenders, as here on Westminster and on my model of Belgravia.

Again she was built from Mike Waldron's etchings, with fittings supplied by John Birch of Albion Models. I use a Slater's motor and gearbox with Slater's wheels and a Zimo sound decoder. For some reason no recordings of a Belgravia seem to have survived (!) so I've used a generic Southern 2 cylinder sound decoder. These were very elegant engines, though certainly not the first to come to mind when Stroudley is mentioned. The last one was withdrawn in 1902.

CLASS A 0-6-0T 'TERRIER'

Probably the best known class of engine the Brighton ever built, the first Terrier emerged from the works in 1872. These tiny tank engines were built for the south London suburban services and the crews called them 'Rooters'; they coped admirably until the larger D's took over.

As mentioned, my engines are all the Dapol ready to run models and a little beauty it is too. My only gripe is that the colour was totally wrong, more of a sandy beige—yuk! However, as I was going to rename my engines anyway it didn't really matter. That's another way of making your layout that bit different—there are lots of Terriers out there, but not many are called Beulah or Southdown. I'll tell you how to do the renaming in the next chapter.

Because I repainted my three Terriers they blend in perfectly with the other engines, so that it isn't apparent that they are ready to run items. The replacement number plates came from Guilplates.

D CLASS 0-4-2T

The next class after the Terriers was the D, which would be built in greater numbers than any other Brighton engine. A D class could turn it's hand to anything, it was true mixed traffic design in the manner of a Black 5 or a GWR Hall. The first of the class was built in 1873.

My model was built from a kit by Albion Models, sold through Roxey Mouldings, and it makes a lovely engine. I chose to model 'Rottingdean' as it is the next village to Saltdean on the Sussex coast.

This was the first engine I built to see if it was going to be possible to reproduce that glorious livery. Thankfully it was, and Saltdean has been the result.

GROSVENOR 2-2-2 & G CLASS 2-2-2

The next loco to be designed by Stroudley was a one off, the single Grosvenor which would develop into the G class. Unfortunately these engines are currently the only ones for which no kit is available in 7mm scale. Sans Pariel did a kit but it was sold on to Ace models and is not currently listed by them. It's a shame because they were lovely engines.

Grosvenor was built in 1874 and was thoroughly tested on the main line before Stroudley committed himself to building more singles. It has 6'9" driving wheels and went like the wind, often working the Royal train. It wasn't withdrawn until 1907.

In 1877 a second one off single, 'Abergavenny', was built which was smaller than 'Grosvenor' with 6' 6" driving wheels. This again was thoroughly assessed and was a highly successful engine, really the forerunner of the G class. She lasted until 1909.

The G class singles did not appear until 1880, so there had been no great rush to produce them. The driving wheels were 6' 6" and twenty four engines were built; having the experience of the two one off engines Stroudley combined the best features of both in the G's and they were superb. The last one ran until 1914, pretty good for a single driver.

It's a great shame that the G will remain a missing link in terms of 7mm loco's, at least for the time being.

E CLASS 0-6-0T

The goods version of the D in many ways, the E shared many components showing the benefits of the standardisation programme. Finished initially in the goods green livery these well proportioned engines were very useful across the system on all manner of freight traffic, though when they were tried on suburban passenger trains during a loco shortage they were less successful due to rough riding. They were introduced in 1874.

My model is built from an Albion Models kit, which just like the real engine shares many parts with the D class.

They were painted green with just a black line when first built but when the Westinghouse brake was fitted a red line was added on either side of the black one. Although these were goods engines they were all named; by this time it had become necessary to look across the Channel for inspiration!

The green livery was done in just the same way as the other engines, with panels of printed paper. An E was quite a big engine for the time; you can almost smell the burning wood from those brake blocks when she's shunting!

D CLASS 0-4-2 'LYONS' CLASS

The 'Lyons' class was really a D class tank without the tanks, if you follow me….a small class of attractive 0-4-2 tender engines that in many ways paved the way for the larger Richmonds and Gladstones. They were introduced in 1876 and fourteen were built. They were really mixed traffic engines before such things had been thought of, capable of all but the fastest running.

The first engines were paired with old Craven tenders but the standard inside framed Stroudley tender was used from No 308 onwards, appearing for the first time and proving to be much smoother riding than the Craven tenders.

Mike Waldron does a kit for the class and it's on my shopping list.

C1 CLASS 0-6-0 'JUMBO'

The enlarged version of the old C class 0-6-0 came into use in 1882 and only twelve were built. They were not Stroudley's finest hour, with a poorly proportioned boiler, but they were adequate for goods work. Old tenders were given to them as the new inside framed tenders were paired with the new passenger classes. Oddly there were twelve engines but only ten tenders so swapping was a regular occurrence as loco's went into the works. The last of the class was withdrawn in 1924.

Again Mike can offer etchings to model this class.

This 'Jumbo' ended up in LMS livery, having been bought from the LBSC by the Stratford on Avon & Midland Junction railway.

CLASS B 0-4-2 'RICHMOND' CLASS

This small class of just six engines was the forerunner of the Gladstones and is often mistaken for one. Introduced in 1878, they had the same sized wheels but a slightly smaller boiler than the better known engines.

This was the class that really proved that it was possible to run express trains using a loco without a leading pony truck or bogie and it was the success of the Richmonds that lead to the Gladstones being built six years later. The superb permanent way on the Brighton main line had a lot to do with it, but nevertheless the sound design of the two classes was obvious.

My model is built from Mike Waldron's etchings and uses fittings from John Birch...with the large inside framed tender she's quite a big engine by the standards of the time.

Just in case you're wondering what she's doing at a sleepy branch terminus just ten miles from Brighton, the works use the branch as a running in turn after loco's are overhauled so I can justify running anything!

'GLADSTONE' CLASS B 0-4-2

The crowning achievement of Stroudley's time at Brighton, the 'Gladstones' were introduced in 1884 and immediately proved a great success...the class was still being constructed when Stroudley died in 1889 and thirty six would be built in all. Clever design meant that they could handle the heaviest trains and maintain high speeds yet still fit on the existing turntables, saving the company great expense in replacing them all.

The Gladstones can be modelled using a kit from Albion Models, and of course it is possible to gain inspiration by looking at the real thing in York museum.

PROBLEMS AND PITFALLS

Unfortunately Mr Stroudley wasn't thinking about modellers when he designed his engines! The 0-4-2 wheel arrangement isn't ideal for a model engine as the weight needs to be kept over the driving wheels to give traction while also keeping the trailing wheel on the track so that it turns.

Generally filling the boiler with lead gives ample weight between the two driving axles and I found that giving the trailing wheel some vertical movement and pivoting the axle in the centre on a sprung beam does the trick. So the beam isn't pressing on the axle and stopping it turning I place a length of brass tube over the axle and the beam presses on that. The trailing axle also needs plenty of sideplay as a loco like a D class had a lot of overhang behind the rear driving axle which was fine on the real thing but can cause problems on tight curves on layouts. For the same reason the drawbar on any of the classes of 0-4-2 tender engines needs plenty of sideways movement.

On tender engines I pick up power through the loco wheels on one side and the tender wheels on the other so there are no pick-ups, an insulating drawbar passing the power from the tender to the decoder.

Mike Waldron's kits were all drawn for Scalefour originally and I have found that clearances are pretty tight so I now use a driving wheel slightly smaller than the scale diameter to give a bit more room. It's not at all obvious and if anyone comments I just say the tyres are very worn! Fortunately the Slater's range is so big there is always something suitable to use.

This is a personal choice, but I replace all the brakes and rigging in an etched kit and make them from scratch using plastic so there is no chance of metal brakes touching the wheels and causing a short—decoders are sensitive and expensive. Plastruct strip is plenty strong enough for the brake rodding and is that bit chunkier than etched strips...the real thing had work to do, it was good and solid. Grantline bolt heads and such like complete the job.

My Single wheeler 'Dieppe' wouldn't run at all at first, she just slipped so I put 'Bullfrog Snot' on the driving wheel tread and now she's fine although only picking up power from the leading and trailing wheels. These axles both need lots of sideplay if she's going to go round any sort of a bend, so I coated the inside of the frames with tape to prevent any short circuits.

LOCOMOTIVE KITS AVAILABLE IN 7mm SCALE

EB MODELS (MIKE WALDRON) These are etchings only and are produced to special order.

Stephenson single (such as 'Dieppe').

Richmond class 0-4-2

C/C1 class 0-6-0

D2 class 0-4-2

Belgravia class 2-4-0.

Mike can offer a range of tenders to suit specific loco's.

ALBION MODELS John Birch (sold through Roxey Mouldings).

D/D1 class 0-4-2T

E/E1class 0-6-0T

Gladstone class 0-4-2

D3 0-4-4T

ACE MODELS

B4 class 4-4-0

E2 class 0-6-0T

H1/2 class 4-4-2

K class 2-6-0

E5 class 0-6-2

A1 class 0-6-0T

J class 4-6-2T

L class 4-6-4T

C2x class 0-6-0

ROXEY MOULDINGS

A1 class 0-6-0T

I3 class 4-4-2T

E4 class 0-6-2T

REPRODUCING THE LIVERY

The one thing stopping more people from modelling the railways from this period is the complex and colourful locomotive liveries.

I couldn't paint a loco in Stroudley livery, and I couldn't afford to pay someone to do it for me so I had to find another way. This was the key question; if I couldn't achieve this then the rest of it becomes irrelevant, it wouldn't be possible to build an 1880's LBSC layout. However, on Saltdean are engines that look like this:

This may come as a shock, but the only yellow paint on 'Dieppe' is on the dome, the firebox front and the wheels. Everything else you can see in this picture is printed on paper, cut out and glued onto the engine.

You're not supposed to finish an engine like this, you're supposed to paint it! On the other hand, if I hadn't told you would you have know that this engine isn't painted? Once the paper has been varnished it looks just like a painted surface. The claret frames are paper too, by the way, and so is the buffer beam. The largest painted areas are the black on the engine and the tender top.

The paper panels are prepared away from the engine using artwork done on the computer. Then they are printed off, stuck in place and varnished. If one gets spoiled it's simple enough to print another and try again, and once the artwork is done it can be used over and over again.

This chapter will show you the basics; I have written a whole book that explains what to do in easy to follow steps so I'm not going to repeat it all here.

Victorian engines may have carried complex liveries but in other ways they are very helpful to us. They have parallel boilers, and usually have round topped fireboxes. They are generally flush riveted and have nice flat panels which are ideal for modelling using paper.

My D class 0-4-2T looked like this when I was ready to think about painting it:

The wheels have already been painted, it's easier to do that off the engine. The cab roof is loose, and none of the fittings that will be attached to the boiler have been added yet, they have to wait until later. Note how I've used quarter round Plastruct for the tank tops, much easier than trying to bend the brass.

Conventionally you'd now prime the loco body, often with grey primer from a spray can. However, doing that means that the paper panels will be glued to the paint rather than to the brass which gives a poorer bond so it's not a good idea. I brush paint self etching primer onto the areas that will be painted, but only those areas. The it's time to turn to the computer to begin producing the paper panels that will decorate the engine.

I use a software called Serif PagePlus which does everything I need though clearly many others are available. I'm just telling you what works for me. I use an ordinary Epson inkjet printer and print onto Epson matt paper, all easily available. I tried gloss paper but the image doesn't soak into the paper but stays on the surface so it's vulnerable to getting scratched. Use matt paper and gloss varnish it later if you want a shiny finish.

That's it really, there is nothing complicated. A scalpel and a steel rule for cutting out the parts and you're ready to go.

This is 'Dieppe' with the first panels attached; I did prime her, you learn these things as you go along. I glued the boiler in place first, as it's the most likely to need doing more than once before it's right...the join is at the bottom of course. Each panel is completely finished before being stuck to the engine using Evostick Impact glue. I find it easier to do the painted parts afterwards, but they could be done first if you want, it doesn't make much difference.

This is the basic panel for Stroudley livery:

It only needs drawing once, then it can be copied and pasted as many times as you want. Making up a tank side needs four of these suitably rotated to make the four corners and then joined together.

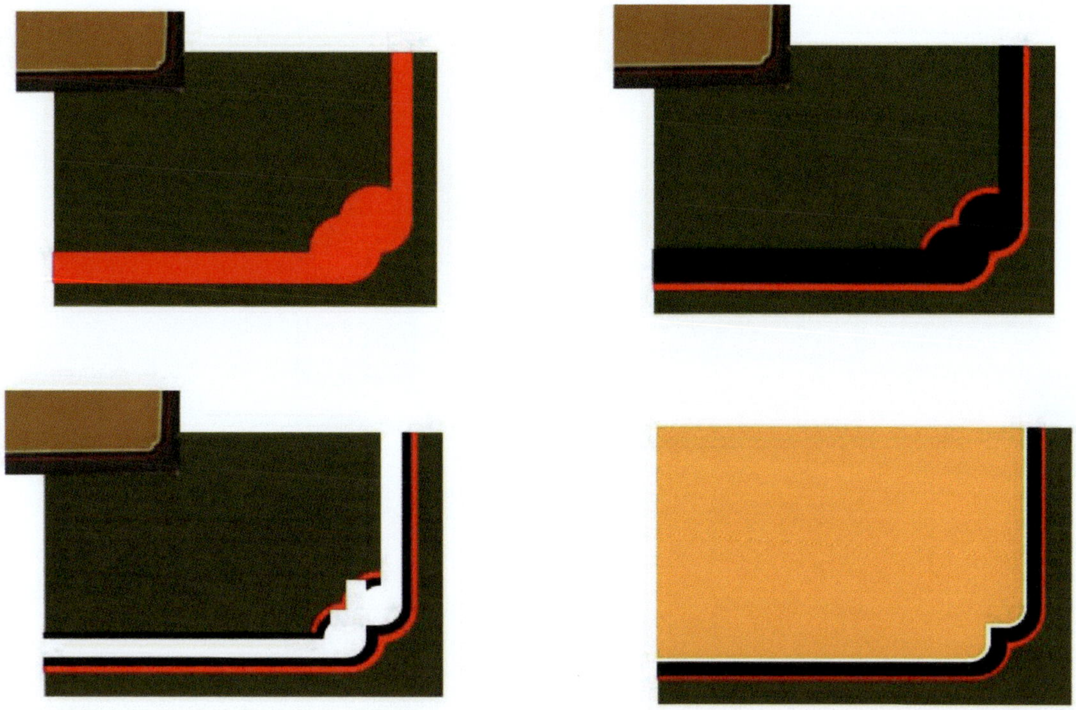

The panel is built up like this, working from the outside inwards; the small picture at the top left is a photo of a real panel for reference which is then deleted. Items such as a loco name can then be added as well a bit at a time:

The real lettering was gold but that's one limitation that we have to accept using this method. For splashers the lettering can be curved, as on 'Dieppe'.

I generally produce a sheet for a loco such as the D class like this:

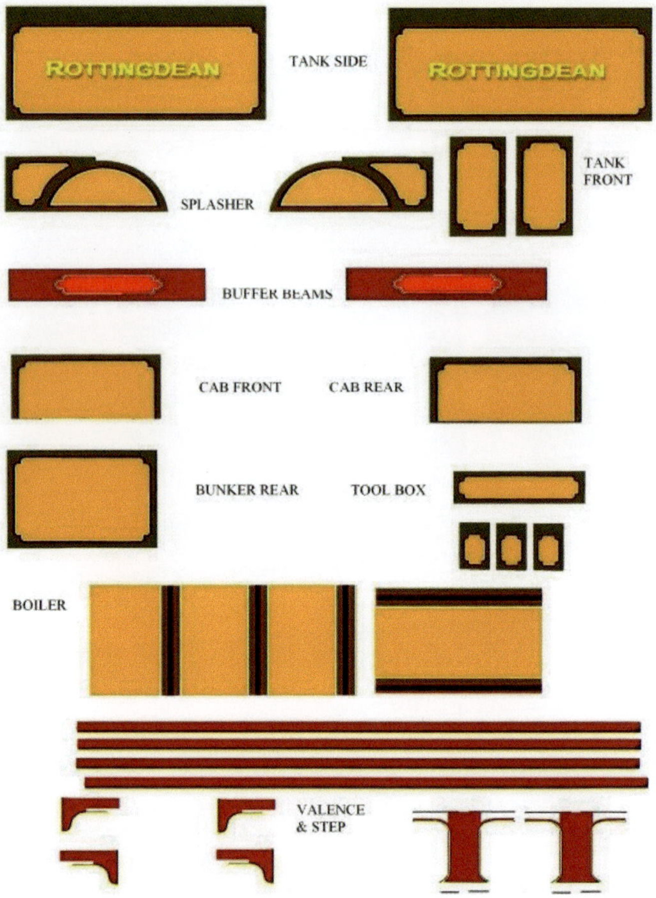

The same sheet could be used for a second D, or perhaps an E in yellow as some were painted.....just the name would need to be changed and the splasher re-done. The disadvantage is that if a piece gets spoiled the whole sheet has to be re-printed in order to obtain the replacement.

This is No. 467 with most of the paper applied and a couple of coats of Microscale satin varnish brushed on. The next stage is to glue in place the castings and to add the handrails.

'Dieppe' at much the same stage. Using glue for the castings such as the dome may seem contrary to good practice but I use Evostick and it's fine, nothing has ever come loose.

The picture below shows how I transfer power between the loco and tender—thanks to John Smith for explaining it to me. The plate on the tender is sprung so there is always a good contact.

One problem can be mixing the paint to match the printed yellow of the paper panels...it's much easier to mix the paint to the paper than the other way round. I use Tamiya flat acrylic paint and begin with a new jar of yellow, adding brush loads of red and mixing it in until I get a good match. Despite all the fancy names, really it's just a yellowy orange! It's better to use flat paint and then varnish it to get a shiny finish. Paint the dome separately and glue it in place once it's dry.

I had to do something a bit different with the Terriers because of course they were already painted. The quality of the paintwork, especially the lining, was superb but the yellow just didn't look right to me and it didn't match my other engines.

The way to rename them of course is to produce a whole new tank side and glue it in place as I've done here with 'Southdown'. The tank tops were painted black first by the way, they shouldn't be green. Then the rest of the engine had to be coloured to match which I did by carefully painting over all the yellow trying to keep inside the lining. When I took the picture her new number plates hadn't arrived.

Terriers were prone to a little staining under the condenser pipe on the smoke box so I added that and toned down the cab roof a little too.

The loco's need footplate crew adding, of course; Andrew Staddon does a pair of LBSC crew which are great but you end up with the same ones in every engine so I also use Omen figures for variety as seen here. The fire irons are from Ixion and Sans Pariel do lost wax brass LBSC loco lamps which are superb. In daylight hours route indicator discs were used which are easily made from plastic card.

All my loco's have DCC sound with either Zimo or ESU Loksound decoders. You can buy decoders with Terrier sounds on them, and of course the Dapol loco's come ready fitted, but for a little variety I have used a generic Southern steam sound on a couple of the engines. Let's face it, no one knows what No 467 sounded like do they?

Dapol produce the Terrier in post 1905 Umber livery too and I couldn't resist getting one even though she can't run on Saltdean. All I've done to her is paint the brake blocks and add coal and a crew.

COACHES

During the 1880's almost all the coaching stock in use had been designed by Stroudley, the old Craven era carriages were quickly withdrawn. Stroudley coaches were all either four or six wheeled, the latter for main line service. Fortunately Roxey Mouldings produce kits for all the commonest types so all is well.

When new the coaches were not painted; being built from Mahogany they didn't take paint well but accepted varnish so they ran in varnished wood until they began to look shabby and were then painted in a brown that was a close match to the colour of the mahogany. A mix of coaches in varnished and painted liveries would be appropriate by 1888 when Saltdean is set, but all mine are in varnished wood simply because I like it.

You can see...and ride in...a Stroudley coach at the Bluebell Railway but it is in the later brown livery, so to see a coach in varnished wood we have to run to the lovely LCDR example that may well be in the same train:

It is very different from a Stroudley design, but it does show how attractive this finish was when it was newly applied with the variation in tone of the wood and the grain running in different directions. All this can be reproduced on our models and in 7mm scale it's worth taking the effort because it does show.

Coaches running on the London suburban services didn't look like this for long; the white roof soon turned dark grey and the sides became soot stained and grimy. LBSC coaches at this period did not receive a good press, they were one of Stroudley's weaker areas though no worse than on the SER or LDCR...sadly that isn't saying a great deal!

This Stroudley four wheeled coach restored at the Bluebell Railway in the painted livery shows how unlike the LCDR example it is, with rounded corners to the panelling. Unfortunately this makes it more difficult to model.

First class passengers travelled in style; third class passengers got a hard wooden bench! It is worth remembering though that people travelling third class in those days were not always particularly clean so upholstered seats would quickly have become soiled.

TEAK 1 MAHOGONY TEAK 2 TEAK 3

We are more used to seeing teak coaches than those built using mahogany, which has a redder hue. I prepared these samples for myself before beginning work on my first coach so I could see the difference and it is very clear. I has a long chat to a gentleman in the carriage works at Horsted Keynes and he showed me the wood they are using in restoring LBSC coaches; it matched this mahogany sample very closely. I added the lining to the samples as the panels on LBSC coaches were lined and it does affect how we perceive the colour.

My first vehicle was a full brake as I didn't have to worry about doing an interior.

The coach was sprayed with Railmatch Light Rust as a base colour, and then each panel was applied separately. I printed them in much the same way as the samples at the top of the page, making sure that the grain runs in the right direction. The panels were cut out just outside the lining and the edges were painted with the light rust before the panel was stuck in place using Evostick. Once the whole side was done it was coated with satin varnish before the transfers and handles were added. The guard's ducket was painted as these were covered in sheet metal.

Because the panels are pictures of real mahogany the coach looks right, much more so than if it had been painted. The lining is inside the panel rather than on the edge of the moulding but I'm happy to accept that. The picture of the mahogany was simply found on the Internet and saved and the lining was over-layed onto it using PagePlus.

This different umber brown livery was introduced in 1905 under Marsh and is not the same shade as was used on painted coaches before that time.

You can't run a layout with just full brake's, of course; my coaches have the interior modelled using printed paper as it is ready coloured, easy to fit and doesn't add any weight....etched brass coaches are heavy enough already. You can't see a great deal through the small windows but something needs to be modelled to give the impression of a full interior. I use plastic card partitions and these help keep the glazing in place.

A brake third coach showing the simple paper interior; it's perfect adequate when viewed through the small windows.

There were no full height partitions in third class coaches.

A first/second class composite—the blue and red material is just flat printed paper but by using a photograph of a real upholstered seat they look three dimensional.

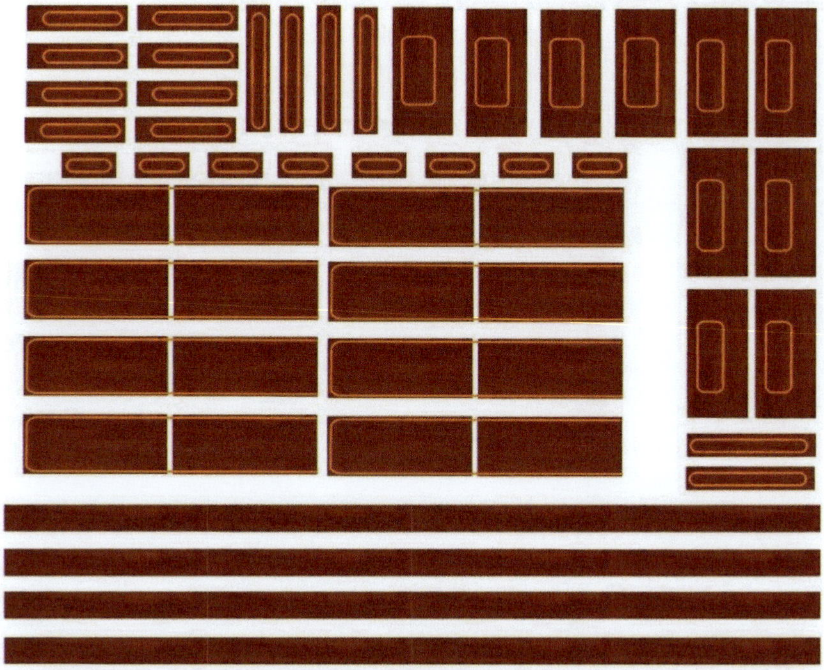

The sheet of panels I used for my coaches.

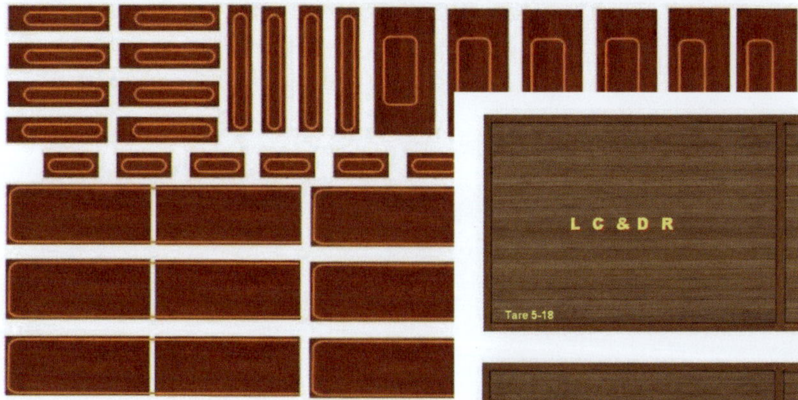

Artwork for an LCDR carriage truck; I always do three sides as inevitably one will get glue all over it!

This vehicle was flush sided so it was ideal for modelling using paper.

The finished LCDR carriage truck, built from a Roxey kit. Coaches generally stayed in their own lines but a carriage truck could well have travelled further afield and it makes a change from the Brighton vehicles. A truck like this was used to transport a horse drawn carriage which previously would have been lashed to an open wagon.

An LBSCR van for use in a passenger train. Built from etchings blown up from 4mm scale it was made available through the Brighton Circle. The wood grain can be seen clearly, the square cornered panels making fitting the paper much easier.

Also obtained from the Brighton Circle, this four wheeled passenger brake van is full of character.

Photographs show that some vehicles ran with white painted wheel rims so I have done that on my models which I think looks attractive.

SUPPLIERS

ROXEY MOULDINGS produce kits for the following LBSCR coaches:

Stroudley 4 wheeled all third

Stroudley 4 wheeled brake third

Stroudley 4 wheeled composite

Stroudley 4 wheeled all first

Stroudley 4 wheeled full brake

Stroudley 4 wheeled mail van

Stroudley 6 wheeled all first

Stroudley 6 wheeled mail van

Stroudley 6 wheeled full brake

Stroudley horse box.

WORSLEY WORKS do a kit for a 60' Director's saloon coach

BRANCHLINES do a kit for a 54' brake 3rd.

RAGSTONE MODELS do kits for five different LBSCR horseboxes.

MSC models did a large range of later LBSCR coaches but these are no longer listed. The same applies to kits once marketed by **ALAN GIBSON**. Kits might be available second hand.

GOODS ROLLING STOCK

Goods stock is not well catered for with kits until you get into the 1890's, when the picture improves considerably. If like me you are attracted to the earlier period you're going to have to do some scratch building, like this:

This Stroudley brake van and covered van are both built from scratch in plastic card using under-frame fittings and wheels from Slater's. Both are really just a basic box with detailing, though the brake van is a bit more complicated of course. The roof is rolled from brass sheet. The finished wagons look like this:

Stroudley used a livery for most goods stock of 'lavender grey', a light grey with a hint of purple. There was no lettering other than on brake vans, but a company symbol was carried with the wagon number beneath it and on the solebar was a cast iron plate again with the wagon number.

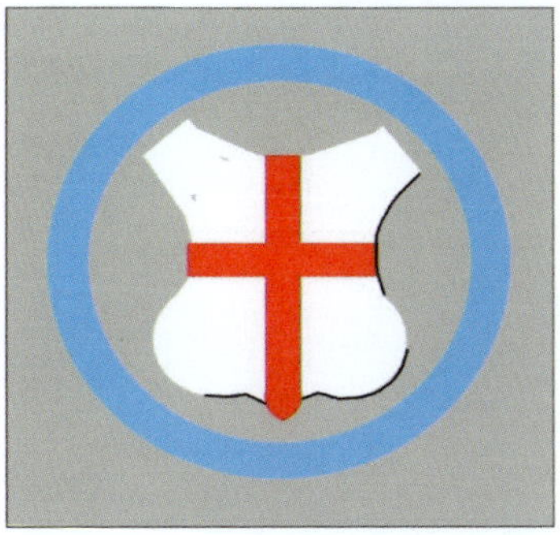

This is the LBSCR company symbol carried on all goods stock; it has been called an illiterate symbol but there is no evidence that this was it's main purpose. In a busy goods yard crowded with different wagons it was simply an easy form of identification, though it does seem rather extravagant compared with the simple white diamond of the LNWR.

All wagons carried this plate on their solebar identifying the company and giving the wagon number and weight.

I model my wagons by printing the grey areas on paper and then adding the symbol and wagon number in white shaded with black. These are covered with a picture of real wooden planks which is faded until the grey below shows through. The black strapping is painted and then the grey areas are cut from the paper and glued in place. The solebar plate is also printed paper; the number has to be correct as it's big enough to read!

The only exception to the grey livery were ballast wagons which were painted red, which is modelled in just the same way. The axle box covers are tissue soaked in diluted PVA glue and then painted when dry.

Those wagons were built from scratch, but of course we need wagons from other railways as well and a few kits do exist. These horseboxes are LBSCR and come from SER Kits as the SER horsebox was virtually identical. The SER van is another of their kits as is the round ended open below. It would be wrong to just stock the layout with LBSC wagons.

These 1860's vintage LSWR wagons were also kits– the long buffers mean they need a four link coupling. With the SER and LSWR wagons all the planking and lettering is printed on paper and stuck in place.

The LBSCR did not have a fleet of loco coal wagons, instead having a contract with Booth Brothers in Nottinghamshire to supply locomotive coal to all their engine sheds. This model is scratchbuilt and stands by the coaling stage; many of the early wagons had the door on one side only and could be turned if necessary on a wagon turntable. Only black and white pictures exist of course so the grey livery is guesswork but seems likely. Booth Brothers went out of business in the 1890's after which coal was supplied to the LBSCR by Stephenson Clarke.

The wagons sides were printed on paper with the planking and the lettering a glued in place after the strapping had been painted black. I've added a Charles Roberts solebar plate but I have no idea who built the actual wagon.

Roxey Mouldings do a kit for a Stroudley cattle van but it is all whitemetal so is incredibly heavy...a train of them would be a real test for a loco. I tend to leave it at the end of a siding as it looks attractive. It is finished in the lavender grey with black strapping.

Private owner wagons weren't as plentiful in southern England as they were in the Midlands and further north but the brewery on Saltdean was the excuse for some PO vans which were used by breweries such as Fremlins and Shepherd Neame in the late 1800's and make attractive models. The van on the left was scratchbuilt and based on a Gloucester Wagon Co prototype while the green van is a kit for an NBR van suitably modified and will run on John Smith's layout North Foreland. As always the sides are done with printed paper; you have to be careful not to get carried away but a couple of fictitious vehicles like this add interest and establish your station as part of the wider system with traffic originating there.

I wanted a proper brick built goods shed on Saltdean but there just wasn't room so we've got one of the small wooden sheds used all over the LBSCR—my story is that the yard was enlarged and a brick shed was built in 1889, the year after the layout is set.

More conventional PO wagons would have been owned by coal merchants and the like who would have obtained their coal from the Midlands coalfield via the Midland railway or the LNWR. I wanted a couple to be based at Saltdean so I came up with these….

I'm not sure how impressed Messrs. Stroudley and Wainwright would be to find themselves demoted to coal merchants, but never mind!

The wagons are scratchbuilt using Slater's underframes, and the sides were done in printed paper which was then cut to fit around the strapping. It was much easier to model wagons without diagonal strapping, which fortunately is fine for the 1880's. Both have Charles Roberts solebar plates, taken from a photograph of a real plate.

If you prefer to use an authentic livery there are plenty to choose from, even in the south of England.

The two brake vans seen here have a raised section for the guard to see along the train; otherwise they are just the same as the van already described. Brake vans always had red ends to make them more visible.

When built these vans had wooden brake blocks but they were later replaced with iron brakes which lasted much longer.

Some very old brake vans could still be seen in the 1880's on workings such as ballast trains, which was all the excuse I needed to model a couple which were built back in the 1840's. The body is all plastic card, with printed paper infill between the panelling.

SUPPLIERS

FURNESS WAGON CO. produce kits for two steel framed open wagons suitable for the 1890's and later. More LBSC items are promised so it's worth keeping an eye on their range and of course they produce wagons from numerous other railways many of which can be used on an LBSC layout.

ROXEY MOULDINGS do a kit for a Stroudley brake van and the horsebox.

The Stephenson Clarke PO coal wagon used from the 1890's to supply loco coal is available from **POWSIDES.**

SER KITS produce the little 1860's horsebox kit.

Other than that you're pretty much on your own, unfortunately. The wagons once available from ABS and MSC have disappeared from the market though second hand kits may turn up from time to time.

DETAILING THE LAYOUT

Just as with any other period, of course, the layout needs all the little details that bring the scene to life. Fortunately in 7mm scale we are very well served by manufacturers who produce just the items we need.

FIGURES.

Sitting in the bright sun at Saltdean station, this little group make a lovely picture. The figures are by Omen Miniatures and I buy them ready painted; I know my limitations and if I can't do something well enough I'll happily pay for something better. Andrew Staddon also does suitable figures for the period and they can be bought painted from Detailed Miniatures. I have to admit that if a figure is described as 'Victorian' that's good enough for me, I'm no expert on the changing fashions of the period.

To put the icing on the cake, Andrew Staddon does a figure of William Stroudley himself!

Group your figures so they look natural; a family group, the little girl and dog annoying the guard, a chap on his own standing by the lamp post. Relaxed poses always look best, and always paint figures with matt colours.

The sooty footprints on the platform where the fireman gets off the engine were copied from the Bluebell Railway, a nice little touch that I'm sure no one ever notices!

The gas lamp should be dark red all over, I need to repaint mine but it's not easy once they're in place.

Figures in small groups look convincing away from the platform as well.

On an exhibition layout whitemetal figures are a problem because of their weight. Just sticking them in place isn't enough because when the layout is transported with the boards on their sides or ends the whole weight of the figure is on that glue joint. Sooner or later it will give way and the figure will fall off and be lost or damaged.

Saltdean is only viewed from the front, so I glue a length of 2mm thick brass wire into a hole first and cut it off level with the knees of the figure. The figure is then glued to the wire so that it is behind them and hopefully out of sight; it supports the weight and secures the figure firmly in place. All the figures in the pictures have this wire, but hopefully it can't be seen. I don't paint the wire because I want the glue to be fixed to the bare metal rather than a coat of paint, though it can be painted afterwards if desired.

It is easier to fix loco crews in place as the engine will be kept upright, but it's still important to think about a natural pose. On a Terrier the crew often stood outside the cab as it was so confined, and here on the E class the fireman is simply keeping a good look out ahead while shunting.

Meanwhile on the other side the driver is taking a breather. The problem comes with a sound fitted DCC loco when you can hear the fireman shovelling energetically but see him standing idly taking the air at the cab door!

HORSE DRAWN VEHICLES

A surprising number of these are available from the likes of Duncan Scale Models, Phoenix and Parliamentary Trains.

Creating your own firms is fun, as on this coal cart.

If the horse is to be included make sure it is firmly fixed, whitemetal horses are heavy things.

I don't depend on just gluing the cart-wheels to the surface, I fix a length of 2mm brass wire into the baseboard and drill a hole in the bottom of the cart into which the wire is stuck. If the wire shows a person standing in front of it usually hides things.

Modelling this period does need quite a leap of imagination—it came as a bit of a shock when I realised I couldn't have a Model T Ford because it was too modern!

Grouping figures around a vehicle creates a nice scene, in this case on the station forecourt. People standing chatting look far more convincing than they would in 'action' poses.

The green pillar box is correct for the period, the red colour came later.

A loaded cart waiting to be unloaded looks more interesting than an empty one would. The bicycle is just about possible, the 'Safety Bicycle' came into use in 1887 so this must have been one of the first in Sussex. A very go-ahead place, Saltdean!

STATION NAMEBOARD

Early station nameboards were hand painted by a sign writer; the familiar boards with cast iron letter screwed in place and painted black and white didn't come in until the 1890's. Boards such as the one I have modelled used a lettering style that was not confined to one company but was seen all over the country and not just on railway signs. The background colour here is cream, with the lettering in black shaded with red but with a cream line between the two colours. Very similar boards were used on the Severn and Wye Railway and there were many others, it was simply an accepted signwriting style in the mid Victorian period. They were used all over the LBSCR, often with the most amazing finials as here which unfortunately are very vulnerable on a model. The cast brackets should be dark red, I hadn't painted them when I took the picture.

The lettering was done on the computer and was stuck to the board after it had been constructed.

POSTERS

Stations were often festooned with posters, and they can be personalised with your station name using Pageplus.

ENAMEL ADVERTS

These colourful additions to your station are very tempting but don't use them on a Victorian layout, they didn't come into widespread use until around 1900. I put them on Saltdean and then had to take them off again! The first factory was that of Patent Enamel in 1889 at Selly Oak in Birmingham, but it would have taken several years for them to penetrate into rural areas such as Saltdean.

OTHER DETAILS

Items such as the flower bed, gas lamp and trolley all add to the scene and all are readily available. The red wooden box with the sloping top behind the lamp was used by the carriage department for storing coach lamps, simple to make but another item that adds to the correct period atmosphere.

An overgrown buffer stop at the end of a little used siding can be effective and is easily done using a mixture of static grass and foliage material.

The other buffer stops are kept clean though, the Victorians didn't let things get out of hand.

SUPPLIERS FOR FIGURES AND DETAILING PARTS.

FIGURES

PREISER produce one set of Victorian figure for 0 gauge and they are superb, but it's only one set—very frustrating. You might not want to use the Prussian policeman!

OMEN MINIATURES produce a considerable number of useful figures which can be bought ready painted.

ANDREW STADDON produces a very useful range of figures, including Mr Stroudley himself and an LBSCR loco crew. Andrew's figures can be bought ready painted to the highest standards from **DETAILED MINIATURES.**

There are figures from all these producers on Saltdean, so they can be mixed quite happily.

DETAILING

HORSE DRAWN VEHICLES. Kits are available from Duncan Scale Models, Parliamentary Trains, S&D Models and others and of course the horses are also available.

ANIMALS: Woodland Scenics produce ready painted cats and dogs, as do Omen Miniatures. Preiser produce a set of sheep with a dog and shepherd as well as farmyard animals.

Unpainted castings can be bought from Duncan Scale Models, S&D and others.

BOXES, CRATES, BARRELS, ETC. Woodland Scenics do some nice ready painted sets, and Skytrex, Duncan Scale Models and others do unpainted castings.

GAS LAMPS. I use the Peco plastic kit which is a bit small but makes up into a nice model. For larger items such as street lamps Duncan Scale Models is the place to look.

PLATFORM TROLLEYS S&D Models.

TELEGRAPH POLES I use the Busch item from Germany which is ready painted and assembled with a real wood post.

BACKSCENES I use the backscenes from ID Backscenes which can be bought printed onto self adhesive vinyl, much easier than messing around with paste and paper. Gaugemaster do a nice range of paper backscenes, some of which were photographed in Sussex making them ideal for LBSC layouts.

BIBLIOGRAPHY

MODELLING BOOKS BY PETER SMITH.

SCRATCHBUILT BUILDINGS THE KIRTLEY WAY

MODELLING SCENERY THE KIRTLEY WAY

STATION COLOURS Details of the colour schemes used on railway buildings.

DECORATING MODEL LOCMOTIVES AND ROLLING STOCK USING PRINTED PAPERS

USING PRINTED PAPERS IN RAILWAY MODELLING. Using paper for architectural and scenic modelling.

These books are all available from Amazon.

LBSCR BOOKS

Many of these books are out of print but all are easily found second hand.

MIDDLETON PRESS I am not going to list each volume, but the whole of the LBSCR is covered in detail and they are indispensable.

SOUTHERN STYLE HMRS PETER WISDOM. The full story of the liveries used by the LBSCR.

LBSCR CARRIAGES Vol 1 and 2 KESTREL BOOKS IAN WHITE, SIMON TURNER & SHEINA FOULKES.

SOUTHERN INFRASTRUCTURE Vol 1 & 2 NOODLE BOOKS

AN HISTORICAL SURVEY OF SOUTHERN SHEDS OPC CHRIS HAWKINS & GEORGE REEVE.

LEWES AND EAST GRINSTEAD RAILWAY OPC KLAUS MARX

THE CUCKOO LINE WILD SWAN A.C. ELLIOTT

THE CUCKOO LINE CRECY PUBLISHING KEVIN ROBERTSON

AN ILLUSTRATED HISTORY OF SOUTHERN WAGONS OPC G. BIXLEY, A. BLACKBURN,

R. CHORLEY & M. KING.

LBSCR MISCELLANY OPC KEVIN ROBERTSON

THE LBSCR THE BENNETT COLLECTION LIGHTMOOR PRERSS KLAUS MARX

STROUDLEY LOCOMOTIVES IAN ALLEN BRIAN HARESNAPE

PORTRAIT OF THE TERRIERS IAN ALLEN HANDEL KARDAS

THE LBSCR THE HISTORY PRESS JOHN MINNIS

WILLIAM STROUDLEY CRAFTSMAN OF STEAM DAVID & CHARLES H.J. CAMPBELL CORNWALL

ROBERT BILLINTON, AN ENGINEER UNDER PRESSURE OAKWOOD PRESS KLAUS MARX

DOUGLAS EARLE MARSH HIS LIFE & TIMES OAKWOOD PRESS KLAUS MARX

LOCOMOTIVES OF THE LB&SCR Vols 1, 2 & 3 RCTS D.L. BRADLEY

29735700R00048

Printed in Great Britain
by Amazon